Going GLOBAL
Beyond the Boundaries

The Role of the Black Church
in the Great Commission of Jesus Christ

To my Dad
Dr. Carl F. Ellis Sr.
(1918–2000)
He taught me to fly airplanes
and encouraged me to soar with my mind.

Going GLOBAL
Beyond the Boundaries

The Role of the Black Church
in the Great Commission of Jesus Christ

Carl F. Ellis

Urban Ministries, Inc.

Urban Ministries, Inc.
The African American Christian Publishing
& Communications Co.

Publisher: UMI (Urban Ministries, Inc.)
P. O. Box 436987
Chicago, IL 60643-6987
1-800-860-8642
www.urbanministries.com

ISBN 0-940955-93-8

Table of Contents

Introduction

I was feeling uneasy as I sat on the top row of the assembly hall at the University of Illinois. The occasion was Urbana '67, the eighth national missions convention of InterVarsity Christian Fellowship, which was attended by 9,000 university students. The previous day, December 29, a number of African American students had an intense discussion at a workshop on ministry in the inner city. We were all concerned about the challenges that confronted us by the outbreak of Black Consciousness and the cultural revolution that followed. These developments had broad implications for the ministry of the church in the twentieth century, yet this convention seemed oblivious to them; that disturbed us.

After the close of that evening's meeting, about a dozen African American students slowly made their way toward me. When they were close enough to be recognized, one of them asked, "Are you bothered by what's going on?" My response was quick and affirmative. Then he said, "We're having a prayer meeting about all of this. Do you want to join us?" I joined them before I finished saying "yes."

We exited the UFO-shaped assembly hall into the bitter cold winter winds (-20º F). We walked about three-fourths of a mile passing Memorial Stadium, and found shelter in a third floor lounge of Scott Hall. After introductions all around and a short discussion, we began to pray fervently that God would raise up ministries like InterVarsity and Youth for Christ in the African American community. Most of us had subscribed to the assumption that the presence of ministries like these indicated God's activity. Since ministries of this type were absent among African Americans, we assumed that God was not at work among our people. Our emotionally charged prayer meeting ended as dawn was breaking.

In the weeks that followed, it became evident that the direction of our lives had been altered. I left Urbana '67 committed to make a difference for Christ among African Americans. However, I was perplexed by what looked like hypocrisy on the part of many White Christians. They were putting tremendous effort into reaching Black people across the seas, yet they did not lift a finger to reach Black people across the tracks. In reaction to this situation, I promoted ministry to African Americans exclusively and opposed overseas missions vigorously. If I only knew then what I know now.

Fortunately over the next few years God broadened my perspective. By asking questions and looking to the Scriptures for answers, I discovered my narrow view of God's presence was way off the mark. Indeed God had been actively involved with us throughout the African American experience. With the help of several African American missionaries, I gained an appreciation for their ministry and reluctantly dropped my opposition to overseas missions.

In July of 1991 I found myself preparing for a short-term missions project in South Africa. This was remarkable because just two months earlier my future was in doubt. Because of a Job-like experience, I had to resign from pastoring a nondenominational church in Chattanooga, Tennessee. In spite of being unemployed, God abundantly provided for the missions trip and for my family for the rest of the summer.

Just prior to leaving the country, "Gypsy Woman" by Crystal Waters was the number one hit on the popular music charts. Once in South Africa, we were on our way to Soweto after landing in Johannesburg. Our driver turned on the radio and to my surprise, "Gypsy Woman" by Crystal Waters was on. I had no idea that Rhythm and Blues had gone global.

My six weeks in South Africa were eye opening to say the least. The kinship I felt with my African Christian brothers and sisters was unmistakable and powerful. Countless times I was asked, "Why haven't more African Americans come to help us?" This South African experience melted my heart about missions overseas and completed my journey toward being a global Christian.

On the way back to America, a close friend and I spent five days in Paris, France. We decided to do some sightseeing in the countryside. So we rented a car. Once on the road, I turned the radio on and to my amazement, I once again heard "Gypsy Woman" by Crystal Waters. From that day to this, I can't escape the thought, "If Rhythm and Blues can go global, then why not African Americans who carry the 'Gospel of the kingdom of God'?"

Chapter 1

Unashamed of the Gospel

"After this I looked and there before me was a great multitude that no one could count, from every nation, tribe, people and language, standing before the throne and in front of the Lamb. They were wearing white robes and were holding palm branches in their hands. And they cried out in a loud voice: 'Salvation belongs to our God, who sits on the throne, and to the Lamb'" (Revelation 7:9–10, NIV).

IN HIS IMAGE

Black is beautiful, and African Americans are magnificent in their variety. Our Afrocentrism is a uniquely valuable cultural expression. However, as Christians, we realize the beauty of our ethnicity is rooted in the understanding that we are in God's image. It is the truth of God's revelation that protects us from adopting a negatively distorted self-image. This truth persuades us to reject false comparison and competition, and prevents us from becoming infected with the same kind of bigotry that we've struggled against for centuries.

Psalm 100:3 reminds us to "Know that the LORD is God. It is he who made us, and we are his; we are his people, the sheep of his pasture." Our identity is not merely a human invention. God has given us the basis of our Black Consciousness and the ability to forge a unique cultural heritage. Although it includes a general expression, the true beauty of our ethnic identity is fully apparent only when seen in light of how God is active in the world.

AFRICAN AMERICAN THEOLOGY

Theology has been commonly defined as the study of God. While I agree with this, I use the broader definition of Dr. John M. Frame: "Theology is the application of God's Word by persons in every area of life."

Theology can be approached from two viewpoints:

1. Epistemology—The study or a theory of the nature and grounds of knowledge especially with reference to its limits and validity. (Epistemology, then, relates to what we should *know* about God.)

2. Ethics—A set of moral principles. (Ethics, then, relates to how we should *obey* God.)

However, it is not enough to view theology from one side or the other. To be truly balanced, we must cultivate our knowledge of God and His Word, and practice obedience to God and His Word in every area of our lives.

Western theology, as we know it, developed under the challenge of disbelieving philosophy and science. Thus, historically, it was mostly concerned with issues connected to what we should know about God (epistemology). It emerged as a *cognitive theology* because it involved analytical knowledge. African American theology, on the other hand, developed under the challenge of oppressive slavery and racism. Thus, it was mostly concerned with issues related to how we should obey God (ethics). It emerged as an *intuitive theology* because it involved innate knowledge. So when we talk about the divide between African Americans and White Americans, it is more than just a cultural issue. It is more than the issue of whether or not we clap on two and four or one and three. The issues go down to theology itself, namely, how we approach theology and how we practice it.

The emergence of a theological perspective in any people group requires two main ingredients: a life situation and biblical truth. Now when I say biblical truth, I don't necessarily mean the Bible in its present text form. For example, during slavery African Americans were not allowed access to the Bible because we weren't allowed to read. However, it is evident that we developed a remarkable ability to transform the basic truths of the Bible into oral form. Therefore, what developed in our experience was an oral tradition that carried much of the biblical truth that sustained us for many years.

At the core of African American culture is a soul dynamic that developed in the context of White oppression and Black resistance. This soul dynamic is the combination of two components:

1. A theological dynamic—The oral tradition that emerged from the early African American church experience. It captures nuggets of biblical truth in powerful phrases and mental images formed from life experiences.

2. A cultural dynamic—Expressions of Black Consciousness that emerge from the roots of our human experience where the image of God cannot be suppressed.

God intends for us to worship Him in our culture. The Bible is meant to be applied to us; it is not meant to be looked at from a distance. Therefore, African American theology is a legitimate expression of the biblical message. This theological dynamic is fully African American, having its historical and cultural application in the Black experience, yet it is firmly rooted in the universal truth of the Word of God.

GOD-BREATHED

The Word of God speaks to every cultural and historical situation. It gives us a transcendent reference point to reflect upon our circumstances and ourselves. There is no life situation whose basic pattern is not already revealed in the Bible. For everything we go through, there is somebody in the Bible who has been through something very similar. Through biblical precepts, principles, and patterns, God's Word provides an adequate and authentic framework in which to view ourselves and understand our cultural history.

In order to truly understand the Bible, we must first know its ultimate Author. According to 2 Peter 1:20–21, the ultimate Author of biblical truth is the Holy Spirit. Similarly, 2 Timothy 3:16–17 teaches us that "All Scripture is God-breathed and is useful for teaching, rebuking, correcting and training in righteousness, so that the man of God may be thoroughly equipped for every good work."

The Gospel of Jesus Christ is, by God's plan, universal in nature (John 3:16–17). God has called His church to penetrate every nation, every culture, and every language with the Good News of the kingdom of God. As we fulfill God's Great Commission, we should always be open for correction, rebuke, and training in righteousness. We should always be open for God to show us that, perhaps, what we've done is not right. One of the main purposes of developing a theological understanding is to learn to see life's situation from God's point of view. We always have to check what we've done against what God says in Scriptures (Isaiah 55:9; 2 Timothy 2:15).

PREACHING AND PRACTICING THE WHOLE COUNSEL OF GOD

The entire biblical message should be practiced and communicated by the church; this is what the Bible calls "the whole counsel of God" (Acts 20:27, NKJV). Since we're not perfect, eventually gaps will appear in our practice and communication. However, when we lose part of the biblical message, a revival breaks out. Revival emerges to bridge the gap and restore righteous attitudes and action in the people of God. In other words revival comes to restore the missing link in the whole counsel of God. Therefore, we must be careful not to become so focused on the revival itself that we will forget it is a link to a bigger picture.

For example, many in the American church have placed so much emphasis on Jesus Christ as *personal* Lord and Savior that we have forgotten that He is also Lord and Savior in the broader sense. As a result we have migrated into preaching a private salvation as opposed to a holistic salvation. When this happens, we end up with a partial Gospel message. Because we have lost a sense of the whole counsel of God, we have less biblical truth than before. Too often the degeneration does not stop there. There are times when a mere revival is inadequate. Personally, I believe we've gone beyond the need for revival. What we really need today is reformation, a true reformation that not only bridges the gaps, but also restores our focus on the whole counsel of God.

SHARING THE GOSPEL

The Gospel is the Good News that God, through Jesus Christ, has provided the solution to the human problem of unrighteousness. By the sacrifice of His Son and the gift of His Spirit, God has provided deliverance from His wrath and is developing in His people the will and the power to pursue His righteousness. Speaking of Jesus, 2 Corinthians 5:21 reveals, "God made him who had no sin to be sin for us, so that in him we might become the righteousness of God."

Righteousness is the fruit of faith. In my book, *Free At Last? The Gospel in the African-American Experience,* I describe faith as:

> ...the proper response to the Gospel, for which God holds every individual who hears it responsible. Faith is a reliance on God's grace alone for the solution to the human problem of unrighteousness, and God's revealed wrath on humankind—a grace that is rooted in Christ. True faith is more than mere belief. It also includes: (1) a complete turning away (repentance) from unrighteousness and all attempts to solve our problem with God by human means and (2) a complete submission to Christ as supreme Lord and ultimate authority. In essence, faith is the root of righteousness (223).

Jesus said, "The Spirit of the Lord is on me, because he has anointed me to preach good news to the poor. He has sent me to proclaim freedom for the prisoners and recovery of sight for the blind, to release the oppressed, to proclaim the year of the Lord's favor" (Luke 4:18–19). The comprehensive biblical Gospel addresses the sum total of all human issues or needs. That is the biblical ideal. That's what we need to shoot for, but we often fail to do so. What tends to happen instead is that we abandon the things the world's system can address, or cover, and we reduce the Gospel to a message that only covers the gap. That's what I call the "Gospel of the Gap." In other words, this limited Gospel applies the Word of God only to those things that the system does not or cannot address.

The Gospel of the Gap only covers the higher issues like meaning in life, eternal life, peace of mind, and those things that the system cannot produce. We allow the system to deliver the basic needs like food, shelter, roads, etc. But when we limit, or reduce, the Gospel to address only life's spiritual issues and allow the system to deliver the basics, in the middle we will have unaddressed cultural issues and needs.

This is precisely what has happened in the African American experience. Those of us who have accepted a solely privatized Gospel tend to apply God's Word only to certain spiritual issues. By so doing, we become further removed from the basic issues that are unaddressed by the system and our limited approach to the Gospel. Unfortunately, by failing to address all human issues and needs, we have lost many people to the Nation of Islam, to narcissism (an egotistic view of one's self importance; vanity), or to other worldly religious philosophies.

We cannot continue to allow the members of our community to fall through the cracks. To bring forth a reformation and restore the proclamation and practice of the whole counsel of God, we must began to do the following:

1. Biblically deal with unaddressed issues, such as dysfunctionality and the lack of empowerment.

2. Engage in what I call "preconversion" discipleship on a cultural level.

3. Help people understand that the Bible does address these issues, because it does.

4. Show them new ways of looking at the Scriptures and approaching theology.

When we do this, people will begin to understand that God is not a stranger to our pain and our concerns. Instead, they will see that our core cultural issues are at the very heart of God's concern for us. This way, more people will be reached with the Gospel.

As we demonstrate our faith by our works, people will see that God is the Lord of all. Then we can expand our communication of the Good News of the Gospel to cover every area of life.

Chapter 2

Suffering and the South

"For there our captors asked us for songs, our tor-mentors demanded songs of joy; they said, 'Sing us one of the songs of Zion!' How can we sing the songs of the LORD while in a foreign land?" (Psalm 137:3–4, NIV).

CHRISTIANITY VS. "CHRISTIANITY-ISM"

When the Gospel is applied in a particular cultural con-text, the result is Christianity. There are many expressions of Christianity because there are many different cultures. Because of our cultural differences, it is not wrong to have a Black Christianity or a White Christianity. Christianity is cross-cultural. However, these cultural expressions of Christianity should never contradict each other if they are true to God's Word. In fact, they will have a complementa-ry relationship as they focus on God's redeeming grace through Jesus Christ. It is this shared foundation of biblical truth that anchors these cultural applications of the Gospel.

In contrast, there is what I call "Christianity-ism." This is a negative form of religion that avoids the truth of God and the true application of His Word. Instead, it seeks to impose its own agenda and carries it out through human effort. Christianity-ism tries to squeeze God into a man-made mold or reduce Him to a system that can be manipulated. It is an attempt to hold the Gospel hostage in an anti-God framework. Although it is preached in the language of Christianity, under Christianity-ism, biblical truth is diluted, polluted, and erased by the paganisms of culture.

THE SYSTEM OF SLAVERY

The dehumanization experienced by the enslaved Africans brought to this country is difficult to imagine. They had been captured, branded, and herded into foreign ships. They survived the long journey of the Middle Passage under horrific conditions that included extreme overcrowding, rampant disease, frequent rape, and fatal beatings. Upon arrival in America, they were stripped of all dignity and power, and divorced from their native language and culture. With physical characteristics that made their identification unmistakable, they were forced to work under a system that seemed impossible to escape.

In *Free At Last? The Gospel in the African-American Experience,* I expose the mind-set behind the cruel actions of the early White slave masters as follows:

> The whole basis of this dehumanizing practice was an illegitimate view of humanity—a view in which skin color determined not only a person's status but indeed the presence or lack of the image of God. It became a time-honored belief among many adherents of White Christianity-ism that the uprooted African had no soul. Black people were therefore classified as nonhuman—in later history as three-fifths human. So raping a female slave was not a crime, nor was it considered fornication or adultery (43).

The use of Christianity-ism to justify slavery is not unique to America. During the days of apartheid, the Dutch Reformed Church of South Africa was also guilty of this. In fact, all who would identify God with only one race of people are guilty of distorting biblical truth (see Acts 10:28, 34; Romans 1:6; 10:13).

SUFFERING AND SALVATION

Since African culture always presupposed the existence of God, African American slave culture became fertile ground for the Gospel. From various sources, many slaves began to pick up bits and pieces of biblical truth. By God's grace, they were able to put these fragments of the Gospel together and derive some interesting ideas. These early Black preachers began to stir the hearts of their fellow slaves as they shared their insights. Thus, slaves began to get the notion that they were created in the image of God. This confirmed their sense of human worth and reaffirmed their awareness that being a slave was a contradiction to their dignity as human beings.

As the fires of revival began to spread among the slaves, freedom from slavery came to symbolize human dignity, the outworking of salvation in this life. The slave masters attempted to suppress the slave revival, but it proved to be futile. So they tried instead to preempt it as they attempted to force on the slaves their own "more appropriate" Christianity-ism.

Slave master Christianity-ism was rejected by most Christian slaves, but under its cover, they began to develop an indigenous theological outlook and practice. As the slaves interacted with biblical themes in their life situation, they developed a theology of suffering.

In the South during the antebellum period prior to the American Civil War (1861–1865), the institution of slavery was king. While volumes have been written about the antebellum period, we cannot find a set of volumes written by southern antebellum African American theologians. For this, we simply have to listen to the oral tradition of that time. In the themes of the Negro spirituals, we hear lyrics like "I've been 'buked and I've been scorned and I've been talked about sure as you're born." Or "Sometimes I feel like a motherless child a long way from home." Or "Soon I will be done with the troubles of the world; goin' home to be with God."

These themes of suffering are prevalent throughout the music that emerged from the experience of slavery in the South. Although many had become Christians, African American slaves never would have come up with a triumphant perspective like "Onward Christian soldiers marching as to war with the cross of Jesus going on before." Why? Because the main theme in their lives was suffering. Thus, they developed a theology of suffering. And it is interesting to note that when we listen to more recent expressions of oral tradition, we still hear many of these same themes.

The southern theology of suffering addresses several core issues that are related to the concept of salvation. The church was seen as a place where slaves did not have to deal with the suffering that so dominated their lives. That is why salvation in the African American church in those days was seen more in collective terms. This view is very similar to the way the Israelites looked at salvation in the Old Testament (see Exodus 14:13).

The theology of suffering was presented in the paradigm of the Exodus. We've heard these themes of deliverance from slavery and oppression many times: "Deep river. I want to cross over Jordan. Deep river. I want to cross over to campground." Or the classic, "Go down Moses, way down in Egypt land. Tell ol' Pharaoh to let my people go." Now we know that they weren't singing about some Egyptian across the water. Everybody knew who "Pharaoh" was. So it was that slaves couched the theology of suffering in the Exodus paradigm.

。。

While the southern theology of suffering also encompasses personal and social issues, for our purposes I want to focus on three cultural core issues: survival, refuge, and resistance to oppression.

SURVIVAL AND REFUGE

The first cultural core issue addressed by the theology of suffering was survival. Obviously, the slaves found themselves in a perilous situation. As a result, survival was a critical issue for them. Refuge was the second important issue. The church was seen as the place where they could escape, to some extent, the domination of the White slave masters.

While it is not always stated, the slave masters did not want their slaves to be exposed to Christianity because of its dangerous ideas. The Bible teaches us that we were created in the image of God (Genesis 1:27), that God has called us to freedom (Isaiah 61:1; Galatians 5:1, 13), and other truths like these. So the slave masters initially resisted the conversion of slaves to Christianity until they managed to develop what I call White Christianity-ism. Then certain teachings, like slaves are to be obedient to their masters, were emphasized and the other basic truths of the Bible were excluded. Of course, these slave masters paid no attention to the fact that the form of slavery that Paul was talking about in Ephesians 6:5 had no resemblance to American slavery.

With this system in place, the masters thought that slaves were pacified by being allowed to have church. But the slaves outsmarted their masters by developing a way of worshiping and communicating through double entendre. In other words, they made it appear that they were going along with the false Christianity-ism, but, in fact, they weren't.

Today I am often asked, "Why do African American

church services last so much longer than White services?" My response to them, "Well, I think the answer is obvious. It is a tradition that began during slavery. What would you do as a slave if you knew that as soon as church was over you'd have to go out and pick cotton? Would you have a 45 minute service, or would it last for five hours?"

Even in later forms of oral tradition, some of the prayers uttered by the saints include lines like, "Lord, make a place for me in your kingdom where every day will be Sunday." This indicates that the church is still considered a place of refuge.

SONGS OF RESISTANCE

The third cultural core issue addressed by the theology of suffering was resistance to oppression. The institution of slavery was so overwhelming that it was virtually impossible to resist it completely. However, many of the slaves began to resist it physically by having church all day Sunday and verbally through the oral tradition. For example, if their masters were present and claimed to be Christians, slaves would sing songs with lyrics like, "Heaven, heaven. Everybody talking about heaven ain't going to heaven." These subtle comments empowered their resistance.

Negro spirituals were the first expression of African American theology. This form of oral tradition and its double meaning was an important form of communication. These old spiritual songs contained both a theological meaning and a message of freedom; they still reveal much to us today.

THE THEOLOGY OF SUFFERING IN THE STRUGGLE FOR CIVIL RIGHTS

The southern theology of suffering can also been seen in

the African American struggle for civil rights. By 1900, most African Americans who lived in the rural South were sharecroppers. Under the thumb of White supremacy, the African American church continued to function on the theology of suffering. This theology was intuitive and ethical. It was a means of survival and a method of coping with the harsh realities of economic deprivation, racism, and social injustice.

Much later in the twentieth century, the theology of suffering continued to carry the southern church. In 1955, Dr. Martin Luther King Jr. transformed this theology from a method of coping with injustice into a powerful spiritual weapon against injustice and segregation. This happened at the beginning of the Montgomery bus boycott.

On December 1, 1955, Rosa Parks boarded a Montgomery, Alabama, city bus after work. She entered the front door, paid her fare, exited the front door, reentered through the back door, and took a seat in the first row in the "Colored" section. This demeaning procedure was dictated by the Jim Crow Law and customs of the day. After a few stops, the seats in the White section in the front of the bus became full, and the bus driver moved the sign that designated the beginning of the Colored section back a few rows. Since Mrs. Parks was now in the White section, the bus driver ordered her to move further back (where there was standing room only) and let a White man have her seat. She refused, the driver called the police, and she was arrested.

In response to her arrest, community leaders organized a one-day bus boycott scheduled for December 5. On that cold and cloudy morning, onlookers watched as the buses drove by with no Black passengers on board. The boycott was a success.

That afternoon, the leaders met and formed the

Montgomery Improvement Association and they chose Dr. Martin Luther King Jr. as their spokesperson. Dr. King then was scheduled to speak at a rally that evening at Holt Street Baptist Church. This rally was held to determine whether to continue the boycott. After only a few hours of preparation and without referring to his notes, Dr. King spoke about human dignity, Christian love, and nonviolence. His powerful message set the tone for the Montgomery Bus Boycott, which lasted 381 days.

In this pivotal speech, Dr. King demonstrated that the theology African American people held all along could be a very powerful weapon to bring justice into their situation. Thus, the southern theology of suffering was used to begin to level the playing field and bring about racial desegregation on public buses and in society.

Dr. Martin Luther King Jr. clearly and consistently displayed this same theology in his ministry as leader of the Civil Rights Movement. It was evident even in his last speech when he said, "I don't know what will happen now, but I've been to the mountaintop, and I looked over and I've seen the promised land. I may not get there with you, but I want you to know tonight that we, as a people, will get to the promised land."

The Good News of the Gospel is that God has provided salvation for His people. This salvation includes freedom and deliverance from oppression. And this biblical truth continues to be good news for all who seek Him today.

Chapter 3

Missions in the Motherland

"Princes shall come out of Egypt; Ethiopia shall soon stretch out her hands unto God" (Psalm 68:31, KJV).

AFRICAN PRESENCE IN THE BIBLE

While it is seldom mentioned, African Americans have a rich African heritage in the Bible. When the Bible mentions Ethiopians, it means black-skinned, kinky-haired people who looked very much like those who were forced into slavery and brought to America. When Jesus stumbled under the weight of the Cross, Simon, a Black man from Cyrene, Africa, was forced to carry it the rest of the way (Luke 23:26). On the Day of Pentecost, people from Africa were among those who heard the Gospel and were converted (Acts 2:5–12). The New Testament church had many African members, including Simeon who was called the Black man and Lucius the Cyrenian (Acts 13:1).

Early Christian scholars like Augustine, Tertullian, Athanasius, and Origen were Africans. Because they were brown-skinned North Africans and not Black sub-Saharan Africans, these theologians were classified as Caucasian by some. However, if these same men were brought to America, they would have been identified as Black.

GOALS OF AFRICAN AMERICAN MISSIONS

Throughout the 1800s, there was a considerable African

American missions presence in Africa. During this time there was also a developing European colonial presence in sub-Saharan Africa, whose interest was primarily commercial. Therefore, they did not pay much attention to the efforts of African American missionaries.

Black missionaries in Africa during this time operated under the banner of what has been called the three C's: Christianity, commerce, and civilization.

Their first purpose was to spread the Gospel of Jesus Christ. A major strategy they employed was to establish Christian communities in the target mission fields. Paul Cuffey, for example, was the first African American to lead such a missionary effort in Africa. He was a wealthy Quaker sea captain and a strong Christian from Boston, Massachusetts. In 1815, Cuffey organized, led, and personally financed the emigration of 38 African American Christians to Sierra Leone, West Africa.

They were soon followed by hundreds of others including Lott Carey and Colin Teague, both Baptist ministers. Later, Carey moved to Liberia where he became a key leader in the Christian community. He was the organizing pastor of the first Baptist church in Liberia, the Providence Baptist Church in Monrovia. The Lott Carey Foreign Mission Convention, a strong supporter of Christian missions worldwide, was founded 60 years after his death in 1828. It bears his name because of the significant missions work he accomplished in advancing the Great Commission of Jesus Christ. Others like Daniel Coker, an AME bishop, came to Africa in 1820 and ministered in Liberia and Sierra Leone.

The second purpose of African American missions in Africa was connected with commerce. These missionaries brought with them an empowerment approach of community development. A major spokesman of this movement was Reverend Alexander Crummell. For him, economic development in Africa was an essential part of missions. He believed the prosperity of Africa could be assured if its natural resources and wealth were properly developed and controlled by its people. Of course, the Colonialists wanted all the resources of Africa for their own countries.

The third purpose of African American missions was to promote civilization. This is where I believe these missionaries fell short. In those days, of course, civilization was defined as American civilization. This caused tension between some missionaries and the African people. However, it must be said that African American missionaries did an outstanding job of promoting economic development and preaching the Gospel in Africa.

DEVASTATING DEVELOPMENTS IN AFRICA AND AMERICA

The mid-1800s witnessed three developments that profoundly effected the African situation. They were: (1) the industrial revolution in Europe, (2) the development of the oceangoing steam ship, and (3) the opening of the Suez Canal (in 1869). With the increased need for raw materials and greater access to them, European colonial activity in sub-Sahara intensified. As a result, the colonialists began to fight among themselves over territory and rights to the vast resources of the African continent. The British were disputing with the Dutch, who were disputing with the French, who were disputing with the Belgians, and on and on.

Eventually, the colonialists got tired of fighting each other. Portugal proposed an international conference to resolve these and other issues. In response, German Chancellor Otto von Bismarck convened the Berlin Conference in 1884 and 1885. At this meeting, the colonial powers carved up sub-Saharan Africa. Sadly, not one African was present at this meeting. The attendees drew political boundary lines that disregarded the tribal and natural groupings of African people.

These changes in colonial policy were accompanied by radical changes in attitude toward the peoples of Africa. As a result, the aims of the African American missionaries were in conflict with the aims of the colonialists. The anti-colonial stance of these missionaries was seen as an obstacle to the commercial interests of the colonial powers. Therefore, these missionaries were marginalized. Some came under persecution, some were jailed, and others were expelled from the colonies. To make matters worse, the colonial administrations denied entry to new African American missionaries.

Within a few years, the entire African American missions movement in colonial Africa was devastated. This also had several negative effects: (1) the church associated missions with trauma, (2) the church suffered missions' amnesia as people stopped sharing our missionary history, and (3) by the early twentieth century, the church gave up on missionary efforts outside of this country. As a result, our missions history was lost inside of a generation and the missions consciousness of the African American church was practically obliterated.

During these years, the status of Blacks in America also began to deteriorate with the appalling rise in bigotry and inhumane treatment. For example, in the South in 1870, if I demanded respect from a White person, I'd get it. However, in 1890, in that same situation, I would probably be swinging from a tree within about two hours, a victim of lynching.

After the post-Civil War Reconstruction period ended, White supremacy was reestablished in the South by various means, including terrorism. Many believed the former slaves had made too much progress too fast. Thus, the southern states created a racial caste system through segregation by way of creating Black codes in 1865 (state laws that enforced racism). After gaining freedom and the right to vote, African Americans were stripped of their civil and voting rights through devices such as literacy tests, the poll tax, the grandfather clause, and terrorist attacks by the Ku Klux Klan. Even the federal government participated in injustice. The U.S. Supreme Court declared the Civil Rights Act of 1875 unconstitutional. In 1896, the high court ruling in the Plessy *v.* Ferguson case affirmed the principle of "separate but equal."

CURRENT AFRICAN AMERICAN MISSIONARY EFFORTS

The late 1960s saw the rise of the Black Consciousness Movement. With it came a renewed interest in our Black history and tracing our African roots. Though it did not catch on immediately in most church circles, by the 1980s, African identity was embraced by most African American Christians. Church choirs began to adorn their robes with Kente cloth. Others began to take a keen interest in the Black presence in the Bible.

The advent of the jumbo jet made travel abroad more affordable and more accessible. Thus, the increased interest in Africa was accompanied by an increased frequency of African Americans traveling to the motherland and other overseas destinations. All these factors and more contributed to a reawakening of interest in global missions in general and African missions in particular.

Today African American Christians are participating in short-term missions in greater numbers than ever before. Black churches across the country are developing partnerships with churches in Africa. Many of us are discovering that the church around the world is anxious to hear our story—"how God has brought us from a mighty long way."

Could we be on the verge of a great missions movement emerging from the African American church? If these are indeed the "last days," could God be calling us to play a key role in preaching the Gospel of the kingdom "in the whole world as a testimony to all nations" (Matthew 24:14)?

It is not enough for us just to celebrate these possibilities. We must act wisely on them. We must learn from wisdom of our forefathers and be willing to learn from those God sends us to. "For this is what the Lord has commanded us: '"I have made you a light for the [nations], that you may bring salvation to the ends of the earth"'" (Acts 13:47).

Chapter 4

Empowerment and the North

"He said to them, 'Go into all the world and preach the good news to all creation'" (Mark 16:15, NIV).

THE QUEST FOR ECONOMIC OPPORTUNITY

The time came when Black people would no longer be satisfied with second-class status in the South. Large numbers migrated to the North in search of jobs and a better way of life. Many think the primary reason behind the Great Migration was the desire to escape segregation and racism in the South. While this reason was important, the real driving force was the quest for economic opportunity.

The life situation for African Americans in the urban North was distinctly different from that experienced in the rural South. Under the system of slavery and the post-Reconstruction conditions of racial oppression, the theology of suffering pervaded the church in the South. In contrast, a theology of empowerment drove the church in the North.

THE THEOLOGY OF EMPOWERMENT

To nullify the effects of daily marginalization, oppression, and messages of inferiority, Black people needed to be empowered with a sense of dignity and purpose. Tired of enduring injustice under a theology of suffering, African Americans in the North began to interact with biblical truth.

They developed a theology of empowerment, and this theology was couched in the paradigm of the Exile. It was in the North that African Americans began to understand that, like the people of Judah, we were exiled from our homeland. It was in the North that people began to talk about the "African diaspora" and draw a parallel to the Jewish diaspora—lasting from the time of the fall of Jerusalem to their return under Zerubbabel (see Ezekiel 4:1; 24:27; Haggai 1:12; 2:23).

Like its southern counterpart, the northern theology of empowerment addressed personal and social core issues as well as salvation by grace through faith in Christ. It also addressed three cultural core issues: human dignity, African identity, and the divine significance of the African American experience.

HUMAN DIGNITY

Human dignity was important for African Americans both in the North and the South, but each had different manifestations. In the South it included the pursuit of freedom. In the North it involved preserving a positive self-image.

As members of a minority group, African Americans in the North were in a sub-dominant cultural position under the White dominant culture. Of course, all standards of what was correct or desirable were based on the dominant culture's European ideals. Consequently African Americans in the North were confronted by thousands of messages each day saying they were irregular and insinuating that something was wrong with them. This created "the only sin is in my skin" kind of mentality. In response, the northern theology of empowerment promoted the understanding that we, as human beings, were created in the image of God. This truth is a critically important aspect in understanding human dignity.

AFRICAN IDENTITY

We generally associate the search for African identity with the Black Consciousness Movement of the late 1960s and early 1970s. However, this movement was based on fundamental concepts that were themselves the fruit of the northern theology of empowerment. For example, in the eighteenth and nineteenth centuries, we generally were referred to as "Negroes," yet most of our early institutions were identified by the word *African*.

Among the early congregations founded under Black leadership was the African Baptist Church in Savannah, Georgia. The first Black Presbyterian church was founded in Philadelphia. It was called the First African Presbyterian Church. The second was called the Second African Presbyterian Church. The first Black denomination was called the African Methodist Episcopal Church. The second was called the African Methodist Episcopal Zion Church. Among the first Black parachurch organizations was the Free Africa Society. Others followed.

Clearly our African identity was an important issue. Why was it important? It wasn't because African Americans thought that Africa was the perfect place. This identity was an application of Romans 12:2: "Do not conform any longer to the pattern of this world, but be transformed by the renewing of your mind. Then you will be able to test and approve what God's will is—his good, pleasing and perfect will."

The northern Black church knew the dominant culture had tagged us as Negroes. They knew whenever you allow others to label you, you also allow them to define you. Therefore, they said, "We are not going to accept what the larger culture is calling us or how they're trying to define us. No, God did not create us as Negroes; He created us as Africans. And we are going to affirm what God created us to be." So the emphasis on our African identity was, in essence, a subtle form of protest.

If you look at this concept a little closer, you discover this response was an early form of Afrocentrism. Although many people don't realize it, Afrocentrism was originally a Christian concept.

THE DIVINE SIGNIFICANCE OF THE AFRICAN AMERICAN EXPERIENCE

This issue of significance can be summed up in the question: "Why are we here?" It is obvious that African Americans were not immigrants. Immigrants never ask this question because they know why they have come. It was their own choice. But our ancestors were brought to a foreign country, not of their own choosing.

In an attempt to discover meaning and gain understanding, Black Christian thinkers asked, "Is there a divine reason why we are here?" They went to the Scriptures to see if anybody else had ever been through a similar experience. They saw that Joseph found himself in Egypt after being sold into slavery (Genesis 37:28). We know from the biblical text that his presence in Egypt had divine and global significance (42:6). Daniel, Hananiah, Mishael, and Azariah were in a similar situation as well (Daniel 1:6). The last three are better known as Shadrach, Meshach, and Abednego (v. 7). They found themselves in Babylonian captivity, not of their choosing. Yet when we read their story, we see that their presence in Babylon had divine and global significance (3:14–30; 4:3–37). The same could be said about Queen Esther under the Persians. Her royal position in Persia had divine and global significance (Esther 4:14).

Christian thinkers began to recognize if Joseph's presence in Egypt had divine and global significance; if Daniel and his friend's presence in Babylon had divine and global significance, and if Esther's presence in the Persian Empire had divine and global significance, then our presence in America must have divine and global significance. As they wrestled with this truth, they began to sense a call from God to take the Gospel of Jesus Christ to the rest of the African diaspora and beyond. This diaspora would include people of African descent in Canada, South America, Central America, the Caribbean, and throughout Africa.

By 1870 the African American church was experiencing explosive growth because core cultural issues were being addressed theologically. In fact this was one of the dramatic examples of church growth in the history of the church. By the late 1800s, there was an extensive African American missions movement. These missionaries had journeyed as far as Czarist Russia. So there was the answer: An important aspect of the divine and global significance of the African American experience—preaching the Gospel of the kingdom to the rest of the African diaspora and beyond.

FREE AFRICAN SOCIETY

An early outworking of northern African American theology was the founding of the Free African Society in Philadelphia in 1787. This was a Christian organization that shared the Gospel message, yet it also had other goals (among them was economic development).

At this time, Philadelphia was a major terminus of the Underground Railroad. Many fugitive slaves were destitute. Thus, the Free African Society was founded partly to help the former slaves to get on their feet. The society recognized the importance of instilling sound economic principles in all of its members. It also provided strong fatherly oversight for fatherless children, especially boys, and supported the sick and the widowed. It was out of the Free African Society that the Bethel AME Church, the first church in the African Methodist Episcopal denomination, was founded.

PAN-AFRICANISM

Contrary to popular thought, Pan-Africanism originally emerged from the African American church as a movement to take the Gospel to the African diaspora. Beginning in the mid-1700s, Black people (including former slaves) from the United States, England, Nova Scotia (Canada), Haiti, Cuba, other Caribbean islands, and Brazil immigrated to various parts of Africa. They went to such places as Nigeria, Sierra Leone, Liberia, and South Africa creating a kind of transnational Black community. Because of the interaction between them, a Pan-African consciousness emerged. The major portion of the leadership in these communities came from the church. African American men like Reverend Martin

Robinson Delaney and Reverend Alexander Crummell were among these leaders. They traveled extensively throughout this Pan-African community and spoke with authority. We will take a closer look at their views in the next chapter.

As other northern antebellum Black Christian thinkers began to affirm a strong kinship with all people of African descent, the Pan-African Movement took root. It helped to inspire the founding of the Free African Society and continued as interest in African identity increased. As a major force in the 1840s and 1850s, this movement helped to shape the theology and early concept of missions in the African American church.

This form of Pan-Africanism is in contrast to the form that later emerged during the Black Consciousness Movement. It had a radically different foundation and philosophy, with roots in secular humanism and Marxism. Consequently, many people today fail to realize that Pan-Africanism was originally a Christian concept.

A THEOLOGICAL VACUUM

The American Industrial Revolution in the North brought massive European immigration and the rise of "White only" labor unions. As a result, African Americans suffered an increasing inability to become part of the "melting pot" and participate in the land of opportunity. In the North, a new kind of racism emerged—institutional racism. Under institutional racism, racial controls were an integral part of the operating practices and procedures of large organizations and the structure of society in general. As a result, African Americans were excluded from the skilled labor force and mainstream American life. Here marginalization (exclusion from the mainstream of society), rather than slavery, became the central problem.

The northern theology of empowerment would have been the ideal basis for the twentieth century African American church to challenge institutional racism and transform the resulting ghetto situation. However, this theology did not survive beyond the close of the nineteenth century. (I will explain this further in chapter 8.) Thus, a theological vacuum developed regarding empowerment and its related issues. By 1910, the explosive growth of the African American church had ended.

Chapter 5

Early African American Theologians

"You show that you are a letter from Christ, the result of our ministry, written not with ink but with the Spirit of the living God, not on tablets of stone but on tablets of human hearts. Such confidence as this is ours through Christ before God. Not that we are competent in ourselves to claim anything for ourselves, but our competence comes from God"
(2 Corinthians 3:3–5, NIV).

"RESISTANCE!"

It remains true to this day that the best way to get the attention of any people group is to address their core cultural issues.

• Richard Allen and Absalom Jones

Among the theologians of the antebellum North were Richard Allen and Absalom Jones, cofounders of the Free African Society. Reverend Jones founded the St. Thomas African Episcopal Church in 1794. Reverend Allen went on to found the African Methodist Episcopal Church in 1816. These two men became the inspiration for like-minded African Americans to break free from their second-class status in White denominations. The African Methodist Episcopal Church was the first independent African American denomination, and Reverend Allen became the first presiding bishop.

• Reverend Henry Highland Garnet

Many people give Malcolm X credit for saying African Americans wanted freedom in this society "by any means necessary." Yet people don't realize that 120 years before Malcolm's statement, Reverend Henry Highland Garnet said something very similar.

Reverend Garnet was born a slave in Kent County, Maryland. He escaped from slavery in 1824. He studied theology at the Oneida Institute in Whitesboro, New York, and then became a pastor. Eventually, he served as president of Avery College in Allegheny, Pennsylvania. In his 1843 address to the National Convention of Colored Men, he stated:

In every man's mind, the good seeds of liberty are planted, and he who brings his fellow down so low, as to make him contented with the conditions of slavery, commits the highest crime against God and man. To such degradation, it is sinful in the extreme for you to make voluntary submission. The divine commandment you are duty bound to reverence and obey. If you do not obey them, you will surely meet with the displeasure of the Almighty....

Your condition does not absolve you from your moral obligation. The diabolical injustice by which your liberties are cloven down, neither God, nor angels, or just men, command you to suffer for a single moment. Therefore, it is your duty to use every means, both moral, intellectual, and physical that promise success....

Brethren, arise, arise! Strike for your lives and liberties. Now is the day and the hour. Let every slave throughout the land do this, and the days of slavery are numbered.

You cannot be more oppressed than you have been—you cannot suffer greater cruelties than you have already. Rather die freemen than to live as slaves.

Let your motto be resistance! *Resistance!* RESIS-TANCE! No oppressed people have ever secured their liberty without resistance (Salley 2001).

• Reverend Nathaniel Paul
People credit Marcus Garvey with the idea that African Americans need to go back to Africa; but over 100 years before Marcus Garvey, there was Reverend Nathaniel Paul.

As the pastor of the African Baptist Society in Albany, New York, Reverend Paul expressed his views in an 1827 speech that became a foundation for the original Pan-African movement. Reverend Paul believed that:

1. The regeneration of Africa was dependent upon true Christianity.
2. African American Christians had a special duty to participate in this regeneration.
3. The day would come when the sons and daughter of Africa would go back to the land of their fathers and spread the Gospel of Christ.

• Reverend James Theodore Holly and Reverend Martin Robinson Delany
As the early Pan-African movement caught on, new leaders emerged. Among them were Reverend Holly and

Reverend Delany. They argued that:

1. The "rape" of Africa and the enslavement of African people could be ended if a strong Black nation could be established in Africa or the Caribbean.

2. The strong Black nation could use its economic, diplomatic, and military powers to rescue Africa and African people from the destructive aims and policies of other nations.

3. The general aim of the movement was the "uplift" and "progress" of Africa. This concept of uplift and progress was based on biblical Christianity. Therefore, missions was a key component of the early Pan-African movement.

• Reverend James W. C. Pennington

The Amistad Revolt occurred in 1839 when 53 Africans were illegally kidnaped from West Africa and sold into the transatlantic slave trade. Amistad was the name of a Spanish slave ship that was carrying these captives to the markets in America. Led by Joseph Cinque, the captives revolted and seized control of the ship. However, the ship was eventually recaptured by an American Navy vessel and taken into port at New London, Connecticut.

This human rights struggle culminated in a case that took on historic proportions when former President John Quincy Adams successfully argued before the United States Supreme Court on behalf of the captives. The courts finally ruled that the Africans should be released and returned to their homeland. In 1841, the 35 survivors were returned to Africa.

During the legal battle over the Amistad Incident, some suggested these Africans should be "educated,"

"Christianized," and sent back as evangelists. Others suggested sending American missionaries back to Africa with the group. The motive behind some of these suggestions was to lay the groundwork for an American colonization effort.

However, Reverend Pennington was fiercely anti-colonialist and refused to have anything to do with colonialistic Christianity-ism. He argued that:

1. The Amistad Revolt revealed how necessary it was to begin missions work in Africa immediately.

2. African American Christians had a special obligation to do "something" about missions in Africa.

As a result, in 1841, a major effort was made to coordinate Pan-African missions on a national scale. Reverend Pennington was a leading spokesperson for this effort.

• Reverend A. W. Hanson

On May 5, 1841, Reverend Hanson argued that the destiny of African Americans was ultimately connected with the regeneration of Africa.

• Augustus Washington

On July 31, 1841, Mr. Washington argued that for too long Africans had been "preyed on by the ruthless hand of European and American avarice and oppression." In the providence of God, it was imperative that African Americans promoted the uplift of Africa through evangelism. He insisted that godly men and women of color must support ministry in Africa. Mr. Washington also asserted that the elevation of African Americans was intimately connected with Africa's future prosperity.

- Lewis Woodson

On August 7, 1841, Mr. Woodson argued that the majority of the world's population were dark-skinned people. Therefore, African Americans had a special charge to go out and take the Word of God to Africa.

- Reverend Alexander Crummell

Today few people have heard of Reverend Alexander Crummell, but most know of W. E. B. DuBois. Mr. DuBois was mentored by Alexander Crummell.

Reverend Crummell began to exercise his leadership in the late 1850s. He was the first president of the American Negro Academy, a national organization of prominent and well-educated African Americans. There is little doubt that this organization and Reverend Crummell inspired W. E. B. DuBois's idea of a "talented tenth."

We have already noted that Reverend Crummell advocated development in Africa and the need for Africa's descendants around the world to develop economic ties with the motherland. He also believed that:

1. These strong ties would lead to the development of Black commercial power both in Africa and throughout the African diaspora (in other lands where Africans live).

2. The God-given mission of African American Christians was to:

– rescue Africa from ruin

– empower oppressed people of African descent

– "destroy the power of the devil in his strongholds" by ushering in light, knowledge, hope, and Christian faith.

Reverend Crummell pointed to the ministry of the AME Church as proof that African Americans were up to the task. He maintained that their success in establishing home missions and founding a college was a model of what we could do in Africa. In fact, at that time, the fourteenth and fifteenth Episcopal districts were already operating in western and southern Africa.

ONE COMMON VOICE

These early African American theologians were advocates committed to the freedom and uplift of their enslaved brothers and sisters in the South. They strongly refuted the southern White notion that slavery was a positive experience for Africans for the sake of "Christianization." They pointed out that slavery and slave master Christianity-ism violated our human dignity, denied our civil rights, and blocked our access to biblical truth and education. These Black theologians argued that what made the African American experience positive was our exposure to true Christianity and education.

Chapter 6

Applying Biblical Truth

"For the word of God is living and active. Sharper than any double-edged sword, it penetrates even to dividing soul and spirit, joints and marrow; it judges the thoughts and attitudes of the heart"
(Hebrews 4:12, NIV).

THE EMERGENCE OF THEOLOGY

As previously stated, I view theology as the application of God's Word by persons in every area of life. God's Word gives us a basic framework to understand the situations we face in life. One of the main purposes of developing a theological understanding is to learn to see life from God's point of view. How can we gain God's perspective on our life situation with a theology done without reference to our situation? While this theology can make valuable contributions, it cannot fully address our unique challenges. We can be thankful for the insights of historic African American theology and today's White theology. However, we cannot continue our dependence on them because they do not adequately address the issues we face *today*. For this, we must free ourselves from "theological welfare," roll up our sleeves, and get busy doing biblically sound theology—a theology that connects with our current life situation.

When life's situations and biblical truth interact with each other, they produce two things:

1. Praxis—The exercise or practice of an art, science, or skill. All of us, whatever people group we belong to, have personal, social, and cultural issues that must be addressed by biblical truth. We must put biblical truth into reality.

2. A biblical paradigm—The identification of a basic biblical pattern that connects with our life situation.

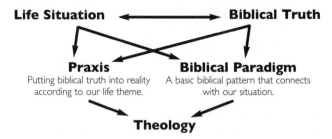

Life Situation ⟷ **Biblical Truth**

Praxis
Putting biblical truth into reality according to our life theme.

Biblical Paradigm
A basic biblical pattern that connects with our situation.

Theology

When praxis and the biblical paradigm interact with each other, what emerges is theology.

The Bible is the revealed Word of God to us. However, the meaning of the Bible is found in its application to a life situation. Apart from this, the Bible does not say much to us. Of course, the Bible does apply in our life situation, but if we don't see it, then we do not really understand it. To apply biblical truth, we must first recognize and understand it. When we fail to apply biblical truth, it's not that the words of the Bible are not saying anything, it's just that we can't hear.

Not only does God reveal Himself in the words of the Bible, He also is revealed in the basic patterns of the biblical life situations. For every situation we go through in life, there is a basic pattern already revealed in the Bible. In other words, whatever we experience today, someone in the Bible has already experienced its basic patterns. Solomon said it best, "What has been will be again, what has been done will be done again; there is nothing new under the sun" (Ecclesiastes 1:9).

DISCOVERING BIBLICAL TRUTH

In order to dig out the riches in the Bible, we must do the following things.

Examine basic biblical patterns. We must prayerfully look for these patterns in the biblical life situations. The key is understanding that along with the words of the Bible, the basic patterns in the life situations of biblical characters are also important.

Match biblical patterns with similar experiences in our own lives. We must prayerfully look for the basic patterns in our life situations and in the life situations of those to whom we minister. Then we must prayerfully match them with biblical situations having a similar pattern.

Take the matchups to the Scriptures. Once we match the biblical patterns to our own lives, we can see the biblical principles revealed. For example, if I know that what I'm going through is similar to what David went through under Saul, then I can look into the Scripture and see how to deal with it. Once we have done this, we can search the Scriptures to discover essentially three things:

1. How was God in control of the situation then?
2. How was God speaking to the situation then?
3. How was God present in the situation then?

The Bible gives all this information away.

We may not understand our situation. We may not know why we're going through what we're going through. But when we look at someone in the Bible who's been through an experience that has a basic pattern similar to ours, we can discover the biblical principles that address our current situation. Once we understand this, we can gain real insight on:

1. how God is in control of our situation now
2. how God is speaking to our situation now
3. how God is present in our situation now

Be inquisitive. Once we have developed this basic theological framework, we can begin to fill in the details. To do this, we need to go through what I call a theological process.

The theological process is based on questions. Jesus told us that unless we come in faith, like a little child, we cannot enter the kingdom of heaven (Matthew 18:3). One thing little children do a lot is ask questions. Likewise, God wants us to be very inquisitive. Knowing how God is in control, speaking, and present will help us frame the issues of our situation. But the finer details come as we begin to formulate specific questions about our situation and ask God for answers.

The development of my book *Free at Last? The Gospel in the African-American Experience* came out of this very same process. As a university student in the late 1960s, I was trying to figure out what God had to do with the Black Cultural Revolution that was sweeping across the country. So I asked God, "Well, what do you have to do with all this?" For the answer, I went to the Word of God and I began to read it with this question in mind. In all of my biblical studies and readings, I continued to ponder this question.

To my utter surprise, I discovered the more I read

Scripture, the more I understood the question I was asking God was not really the correct one. Since the Word of God is "useful for teaching, rebuking, correcting and training in righteousness" (2 Timothy 3:16), the Word of God began to correct my question. The more I studied, the more I began to understand the question was not "What does God have to do with the Black cultural revolution?" but "What does the revolution have to do with God?" So my question was corrected.

Next, as we meditate on God's Word and the corrected question, God gives us answers. He begins to show us things that we've never seen before and in doing so, He answers our questions. Then we must come back to our situation and apply those answers. As we apply God's answers to our situation, two things happen.

1. It causes us to produce a theology that's appropriate for our situation and speaks to its issues.

2. It causes new questions to arise. We take these new questions back to God, get them corrected, and go through the process all over again.

THE THEOLOGICAL PROCESS

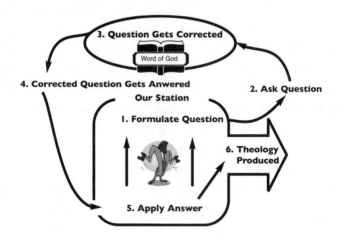

PARABLES AND ILLUSTRATIONS IN THE BIBLE

Now the Bible itself uses this technique of basic patterns. You see this in the parables and illustrations of Jesus, the apostles, and the prophets. You also see this in the books of Proverbs and Ecclesiastes. Through basic patterns of life, the Bible teaches us wisdom.

Of course, a classic example of this is found in 2 Samuel 12:1–13. After David slept with Bathsheba and had her husband Uriah killed, he thought he had everything covered up. Then the prophet Nathan came to confront him. Nathan asked David to make a judgment about a story. The prophet began to elaborate about a rich neighbor who had many sheep and his poor neighbor who had one little lamb. One day, the rich neighbor had company and he took the lamb from the poor neighbor, slaughtered it, and served it to his guest. Upon hearing the story, David was angry. He said a man like that should die. Nathan just pointed him out and said, "You are the man. You've done the exact same thing." Nathan explained what David had done with Bathsheba (a rich man robbing a poor man, stealing and killing what did not belong to him) was like the man in the story.

Many times a modern translation of the Bible can be very helpful at this point. When we read the Word of God in the language we speak every day, often the subtleties will become clearer and the principles more easily discerned.

SUPPLYING THE DETAILS

Often in Bible narratives, many of the details of the original life situation are purposefully omitted. Why? Because the Bible is designed for us to get into those patterns and supply details from our own lives.

Finally, in every theological process, God Himself must have the final say. We should always be open for correction and rebuke, and allow God to show us that, perhaps, what we've done is not right. His ways are not our ways (Isaiah 55:9). We always have to check what we've done against what God says in Scripture.

The Bible can provide a basic framework for understanding our current situation. The main purpose of the theological process is to develop a framework to understand our situation by learning how to see it from God's point of view. After doing this, then we begin to fill in the details inside the frame.

Dr. Henry Mitchell has said that the Bible is like powdered milk: It has all the ingredients of whole milk, but it would be difficult to drink in its present form. I suppose a person could spoon powdered milk into their mouth and get all the nutrients that way. However, God's Word becomes most useful and goes to work in us when we apply the water of our lives to it.

Consequently the Bible is meant to be applied to us; it's not meant to be spiritual knowledge that is disconnected from application. God wants us to get into His Word to understand our situations from His point of view and to govern our responses according to His principles. This is how we will gain wisdom. If we wisely apply the Word of God to our life situations, we will make a difference in our community.

The African American community today is in desperate need of a fresh approach to theology—a theology that is true to Scripture and, at the same time, speaks to our current situation. It is very important that we understand that God speaks to us in many ways in the Bible, and one important way is through its basic patterns. Now if we approach theology this way, the Word of God will come alive and speak to us not just in the "sweet by and by," but also in the "nasty now and now."

Chapter 7

Called to Righteousness— Transcending the Culture

"But you, man of God, flee from all this, and pursue righteousness, godliness, faith, love, endurance and gentleness. Fight the good fight of the faith. Take hold of the eternal life to which you were called when you made your good confession in the presence of many witnesses" (1 Timothy 6:11–12, NIV).

CULTURAL UNRIGHTEOUSNESS

Culture is a critical component of a people's sense of history and destiny. It has been defined as the patterned way in which people do things together. However, visible actions are more a manifestation of culture than culture itself. Culture is composed of commitments, values, and beliefs about the world and people. When basic underlying cultural principles do not include God, the entire culture will end up with a distorted view of reality, and godlessness will affect every area of life.

The African American community today is in serious need of a fresh examination of our culture. In the context of the current cultural crisis, unrighteousness assaults us from all sides. Its powerful impact is most visible in our younger generation. Countless children are being lost to the practices of humanism (a way of life centered on human interests or values), hedonism (a doctrine of pleasure viewed as the primary good in life), nihilism (thug mentality), and materialism (a preoccupation with material things over spiritual things). This is unacceptable. We must rescue our youth with a strong biblically based world and life view. We must also equip them with theological tools to enable them to positively impact our culture and overcome the unrighteous assaults they face.

It is only by seeing ourselves as God sees us will we be able to avoid negative values and self-destructive behavior. Efforts to repair culture based upon a secularist worldview will eventually degenerate and fall apart because it is an inadequate foundation. The secularist notion that we can be independent from God denies the reality of God's lordship, and any effort based on denial can never succeed. To successfully reconstruct our African American culture, we must build upon the standards and values contained in the Word of God.

COMPONENTS OF UNRIGHTEOUSNESS

Whenever people lack a basic commitment to God, unrighteousness follows. Both righteousness and unrighteousness are covenantal and relational terms. The covenant itself is best expressed in God's statement, "I will be your God and you will be my people" (Leviticus 26:12; Jeremiah 7:23; 11:4; 30:22). A simple definition of unrighteousness, biblically speaking, is a failure to do right by the other party in the covenant.

Scripture identifies at least four dimensions of unrighteousness. I call them: *ungodliness* and *oppression* as expressed in the *individual* dimension and the *institutional* dimension.

Ungodliness happens when a person sins and suffers his or her own consequences. Oppression happens when a person sins and forces others to suffer the consequences or when a person tries to force his or her sin on others. These unrighteous behaviors are expressed in the individual dimension by face-to-face intentional sin. They are expressed in the institutional dimension through sin that is woven into the structure and social fabric of society; this type of sin does not need the intention or the consciousness of the individual to have an effect on its victims.

By pairing these dimensions, we end up with four manifestations of unrighteousness as illustrated in the figure below.

THE WINDOW OF UNRIGHTEOUSNESS

Individual Ungodliness	Institutional Ungodliness
Individual Oppression	Institutional Oppression

EXAMPLES OF UNRIGHTEOUS ACTION

• *Individual Ungodliness*

When we lie, cheat, or steal, we manifest individual ungodliness, and it can have far-reaching effects. An infamous illustration of this came in the O. J. Simpson trial (January–October 1995). Mark Fuhrman, the lead police detective in the case, testified that he found incriminating evidence on Simpson's property. In the course of the trial, Fuhrman was accused of being a racist. Under cross-examination in this racially charged case, Fuhrman emphatically stated that he was not a racist. Later, the jury heard taped excerpts from a 1988 interview in which Fuhrman was clearly heard referring to African Americans as "niggers." Not only did this discredit Fuhrman's testimony, it severely damaged the prosecution's case.

• *Individual Oppression*

When we harass, bully, or ridicule others, we commit acts of individual oppression. As a pastor I dealt with scores of people whose lives were adversely affected by the abuse their parents inflicted on them. In too many cases these negative effects were passed down to succeeding generations. The apostle Paul warns us about parental abuse, "Fathers, do not embitter your children, or they will become discouraged" (Colossians 3:21). J. B. Phillips translates it, "...don't overcorrect your children, or they will grow up feeling inferior and frustrated."

• *Institutional Ungodliness*

The activity of the National Gay and Lesbian Task Force is a good example of institutional ungodliness. This is a whole community of people who have made a lifestyle choice that is immoral. They pursue it as if it is legitimate and insist that the rest of society must accept their lifestyle.

● *Institutional Oppression*

The sharecropper system is a clear example of institutional oppression. In the rural South, being a tenant farmer was often the only means of survival. The landowner had the only source of food, clothing, shelter, and farming supplies in his possession. Thus, sharecroppers had to obtain these things from the landowner on credit, to be paid in full out of the proceeds from the harvest. Typically, the sharecropper kept from one-half to four-fifths of the yield from his cash crops. He received his share from the landowner in a "settling-up" at the end of the harvest. However, the money that the share cropper made seldom covered his debt. The landowner usually inflated the amount he charged his tenants for what he supplied, and minimized what he paid them for their cash crops. The state and local laws favored the landowners.

The plight of many Appalachian coal minors was the same. In the mid 1950s, Tennessee Ernie Ford depicted this in his hit song "Sixteen Tons." The chorus goes:

"You load sixteen tons, and what do you get?
Another day older and deeper in debt.
St. Peter don't you call me 'cause I can't go.
I owe my soul to the company store."

For me, the most vivid example of institutional oppression involved my father, an original Tuskegee Airman. He and his cohorts flew P-51 Mustangs and escorted bombers over the European theater in World

War II. They amassed an outstanding combat record, i.e., they never lost a bomber to enemy fighters.

His goal was to be an airline pilot upon his return after the war. However, in spite of his superior flying skills, the airlines never considered his applications. Their reasons went something like this: "People will never accept a Negro pilot. If you fly for us, we'll lose passenger loyalty. Please understand, we have nothing against you. It's not personal. It's just business."

One reason the church has failed to address the cultural issues of our day is because we tend to focus only on individual ungodliness. As a result, when we encounter the institutional oppression that we've experienced for far too long, we have nothing to say about it and we are unable to show how Scripture addresses it. If the whole window of unrighteousness represents the Great Commission, then we perhaps have withdrawn from three-fourths of it. To affect cultural unrighteousness, we must begin to address every issue we face biblically.

COMPONENTS OF RIGHTEOUSNESS

In my book, *Free at Last? The Gospel in the African-American Experience*, I describe righteousness as:

> the perpetual pursuit of God and His revelation in every area of life, both individually and corporately. It consists of seeking to live by the principles of the kingdom of God—principles that manifest themselves in [biblical values] such as...equality, integrity, compassion, grace, and love (261).

A simple description of righteousness, biblically speaking, is to do right by the other party in the covenant. The Bible identifies at least four dimensions of righteousness. I call them: *godliness* and *justice* as expressed in the *personal* dimension and the *social* dimension.

Godliness consists of doing right by God; it usually involves devotion and piety. Justice consists of doing right by our fellow human beings; it usually involves freeing people from unjust situations and helping them to do the right thing. These righteous behaviors are expressed in the personal dimension by doing right on a one-on-one basis. They are expressed in the social dimension by doing right corporately as a society.

By pairing these dimensions, we end up with four manifestations of righteousness as illustrated in the figure below.

THE WINDOW OF RIGHTEOUSNESS

Personal Godliness	Social Godliness
Personal Justice	Social Justice

EXAMPLES OF RIGHTEOUS ACTION
• *Personal Godliness*

When we "say grace" before we eat or have daily devotions, we demonstrate personal godliness.

• *Personal Justice*

When we as individuals participate in activities that free people from bad circumstances or improve the quality of their lives, we demonstrate personal justice. This can consist of things like being a mentor to someone who needs the life skills we have, helping the unemployed find gainful employment, developing a fatherly relationship with fatherless children, etc.

• Social Godliness

During the mid-1980s, several top musical entertainers responded to a famine in Africa by producing a hit recording entitled "We Are the World." The proceeds from the sale of this record went to a special famine relief fund. These artists did not claim to be Christians. Yet, they were motivated by a sense of compassion for others who were less fortunate. This example of social godliness inspired similar efforts by many other countries.

• Social Justice

One of the best examples of social justice was the effect the Civil Rights Movement had on this country. While it did not solve all of America's social ills, it did have a positive effect on countless millions, both here and abroad.

In the Christian community in America, our inadequate view of righteousness tends to focus only on personal godliness. If the whole window of righteousness represents the Gospel, then perhaps we have neglected three-fourths of it. While personal godliness or piety is a good thing, it falls far short of the complete righteousness God calls us to be about. Our failure to demonstrate righteousness, especially the areas of personal and social justice, has caused us to have an inadequate and oftentimes irrelevant theology. To exercise a theology that is appropriate and biblical, we must, by God's grace, display all four manifestations of righteousness.

Here are a few general observations about the windows of righteousness and unrighteousness. Each pane of these windows is dependent upon the other three panes for support. If one section is removed or broken, the integrity of the whole window is compromised. The removal of each additional pane further degrades the window's integrity, and ultimately the last pane left will be stressed to the breaking point and lost.

Consequently we, as the body of Christ, must address all four manifestations of unrighteousness with the Word of God. We must also practice all four manifestations of righteousness by the power of the Holy Spirit. If we limit ourselves to only the scope of personal godliness and individual ungodliness, we will end up failing in these areas also.

THE RIGHTEOUSNESS OF GOD

God is the God of righteousness and justice (Psalm 89:14; 116:5). He has compassion and love for people (Psalm 86:15; 1 John 1:10). The righteousness of God made available to us through faith in Jesus Christ sets us free from sin. It is by God's grace alone that we have the power and the will to demonstrate righteousness and resist unrighteousness. When God is left out, so is His special grace. And without God's grace, we lose the very possibility of both righteousness and true freedom.

A godly form of justice is illustrated in the Jubilee principle in Leviticus 25:10–17. Here God says, "Consecrate the fiftieth year and proclaim liberty throughout the land to all its inhabitants. It shall be a jubilee for you; each one of you is to return to his family property and each to his own clan" (v. 10). When the Israelites inherited the land of Canaan, God gave every family a parcel of land, and they were free to buy and sell as they pleased. Although many prospered, others went broke, suffered oppression, or experienced misfortune. Those who had no means of survival had the option of selling themselves to their neighbors as "slaves." At the end of six years, the "slaves" were to be freed and given a large farewell present (Deuteronomy 15:12–15).

In the year of Jubilee at the end of a fifty-year period, all land would revert to the original owner and all debts would be cancelled. All slave contracts would be cancelled also. That's why it was called the year of Jubilee. This biblical economic example illustrates God's concern for human liberation and empowerment.

Israel never practiced the Jubilee principle. Therefore, they became a society marked by all four manifestations of unrighteousness. God judged them for their disobedience by sending them into Babylonian exile for 70 years to make up for the Jubilee years they ignored.

The freedom to obey God and the power do what is right in His sight is the ultimate freedom. John 8:36 teaches us "if the Son makes you free, you will be free indeed." Human freedom comes from God. Therefore, as African Americans, our search for liberation is not a search for freedom from God, but a search for freedom in God. Apart from the pursuit of righteousness, true liberation is impossible.

The pursuit of righteousness must become the top priority of the African American Christian agenda if we are to become the people God created us to be (Matthew 6:33). When we move forward in this pursuit, we will have the kind of cultural and spiritual revolution we've needed for a long time. It would help us to understand why God has us here in the first place and propel us to take our rightful place in the unfolding purposes of God in the world.

Chapter 8

Traditional Models of African American Churches

"Keep watch over yourselves and all the flock of which the Holy Spirit has made you overseers. Be shepherds of the church of God, which he bought with his own blood" (Acts 20:28, NIV).

THE CHANGING COURSE OF CHURCH HISTORY

Prior to the Civil War, the African American church held two parallel theologies: the southern theology of suffering, which was based on the paradigm of the Exodus, and the northern theology of empowerment, which was based on the paradigm of the Exile.

Great gains were made in the years immediately after the Civil War. The abolition of slavery and post-Civil War Reconstruction set the stage for astounding economic, political, and social progress by African Americans. As the Exodus paradigm was being realized, the need for the theology of suffering began to decline. African Americans were, in fact, coming out of slavery ("Egypt"). As a result, the southern church abandoned the theology of suffering and adopted the northern church's developing theology of empowerment.

During this time, self-help societies, modeled on the Free African Society, proliferated throughout the South.

Among them were The Rising Star, The Sisters of Love, The Daughters of Bethel, Love and Charity, Builders of the Walls of Jerusalem, Brothers and Sisters of Esther, Brothers and Sisters of Charity, and Brothers and Sisters of Love. All these societies were based on the theology of empowerment. Another result was the rapid expansion of African American missions in Africa. In addition, as core cultural issues were addressed theologically, the explosive growth of the African American church between 1870 and 1910 has remained, thus far, unparalleled in American history.

TRAUMATIC EVENTS

Three traumatic events occurred between 1875 and 1900 that changed the course of the African American church: (1) the end of the post-Civil War Reconstruction of the South; (2) the industrial revolution in the North; and (3) the consolidation of European colonialism over sub-Saharan Africa.

1. The End of the Post-Civil War Reconstruction in the South

The final death blow to the Reconstruction came in 1877, when President Rutherford B. Hayes removed federal troops from the South that were enforcing the Fourteenth and Fifteenth Amendments. As a result, Jim Crow backlash occurred and, as I discussed in chapter 3, White supremacy was reestablished throughout the South. In the wake of these events, a new type of slavery was established—the sharecropper system.

2. The Industrial Revolution in the North

After the Civil War, America experienced a significant growth in jobs due to the Industrial Revolution. Looking for opportunity, former slaves were the ideal candidates to become members of the skilled labor force in the emerging industries in the North. However, many Northern industrialists were racists like those in the South, and they did not want to have a large African American workforce. This period saw a wave of massive European immigration, which many industrialists encouraged. From this workforce emerged White-only labor unions.

Along with the rise in immigration came the need to Americanize all immigrants who spoke different languages and had different cultures. To encourage people to assimilate into what the dominate culture defined as American culture, "the melting pot" concept was promoted. However, this concept did not advocate a true melting pot because it did not include elements of all the different and diverse cultures. Instead, it was based on British or Anglo-Saxon Protestant standards. In essence, the closer you were to these White standards, the easier it was for you to "melt," or blend in. Therefore, those who had greater difficulty "melting" ended up being confined to urban ghettos, e.g., "the Black belt" ("the hood"), Chinatown, Jew town, little Italy, the barrio.

The end result was that African Americans in both the North and South were excluded from the skilled labor force and from mainstream American life. With the dawning of the twentieth century, Black Americans saw the development of institutional racism that was structural, systemic, and not always obvious.

3. The Consolidation of European Colonialism over Sub-Saharan Africa

In chapter 3, I pointed out that as European rule spread over Africa, African American missionaries were persecuted, pushed out, and excluded from the colonies. As a result, our missions movement was decimated and largely forgotten by the church.

The African American church was caught off guard by these traumas. As concern for survival again became the overwhelming issue, the developing theology of empowerment was abandoned by 1900. The church reverted to the theology of suffering that developed during slavery. The result, as I stated in chapter 3, was a theological vacuum pertaining to empowerment and its related concerns.

THREE MODELS OF THE TRADITIONAL CHURCH

The remaining theology of suffering proved to be inadequate for the harsh realities of the urban North, especially the experience of ghetto life. Thus, the church slid into a non-transformative function, and its ability to influence the culture weakened. As the traditional church attempted to cope with these new realities, three basic models developed: the *separational* model, the *sociological* model, and the *associational* model.

1. The Separational Model

The separational model was based on intuitive theology. It represented one theological extreme. It sought to protect its people from the corruption of the surrounding urban culture. Congregations of this model were usually very small and held services every night. In essence, these churches functioned as a fortress, keeping the

world out and keeping its members in. It was character-
ized by an inside language unique to these church circles,
where phrases like, "When I was in the world..." were
common.

The strength of the separational model was that it provided a comfort zone in the midst of the impersonal realities of the urban North. People in these churches tended
to come from the same towns in the rural South. Its
weakness was that the primary focus of its preaching and
teaching was separation—separation from this, and separation from that—in order to maintain a life of "holi-
ness." Thus, it cut itself off from having any significant
impact on African American culture.

2. The Sociological Model

The sociological model was marginally based on intuitive theology. It represented the other extreme by primarily seeking to engage the surrounding urban culture.
Congregations of this model tended to be large with a
high percentage of educated and professional people.
Their Sunday services ranged from long and emotional to
short and unemotional. The social outworking of the
Bible was seen as more important than the Bible itself. In
essence, these churches functioned as a social service
agency or a political base.

The strength of the sociological model was that it was
influential in improving life in the ghetto, mostly in the
areas of housing, employment, and education. Its weakness was that its influence was nontheological.

3. The Associational Model

The associational model was based on intuitive theology. It represented a middle perspective. It sought to "keep hope alive" in its people by reminding them of how God's covenant faithfulness applies to what they are going through in the present. Their Sunday services resembled those of he sociological churches. When people think of the "typical Black church," they tend to think of this model. In essence, these churches functioned as a religious club.

The strength of the associational model was that it kept its members going from week to week and helped preserve the theological dynamic. Its weakness was that, apart from church culture, it seldom ministered to the surrounding community.

TRADITIONAL CHURCH PROFILES

	Separational Model	Sociological Model	Associational Model
Northern churches	25%	25%	50%
Southern churches	5%	5%	90%

The northern and southern traditional Black churches had slightly different profiles, primarily because their models had different proportions (see the profiles in the chart above). Also, after 1955, the southern church was able to play a more transformative role than its northern counterpart because it shared the theology of suffering with the Civil Rights Movement.

ALTERNATIVE APPROACHES TO CULTURAL TRANSFORMATION

Because these churches were non-transformative, they were unable to produce significant positive change in the culture. Hence, change began to occur more and more outside of the reach of the church. By 1910 the church was no longer growing at an explosive rate.

The attempts to fill the theological vacuum can be placed into two general categories: *alternative theologies* of empowerment and *ideologies* of empowerment.

• *Alternative Theologies of Empowerment*

Soon after the church stopped addressing cultural core issues, several alternative theologies became popular. Black Jewish sects developed. Generally, they concluded that the Jews were Black because they were non-White. And since Jews were the "chosen people," then Black peo-ple were the chosen people. Several of these sects were moderately successful.

Another alternative theology came with the rise of the Garvey Movement (the United Negro Improvement Association with its now familiar colors of red, black, and green). Reacting to White "Christianity-ism," Marcus Garvey believed that Blacks would never find justice in this country. He concluded that Black unity could be accomplished only on the basis of a Black god, and Black peoples of the world need to unite into a Black nation in Africa.

The third and, by far, most successful alternative theologies were those of the Black Nationalist Islamic sects. The first was the Moorish Science Temple Divine and National Movement of North America. It was started by a man named Timothy Drew who later changed his name to

Nobel Drew Ali. Of the 16 major Islamic sects in the African American community today, about 12 or 13 of them can directly or indirectly trace their roots back to the Moorish Temple of Science. Some factions, like the six groups that call themselves "Nation of Islam," espouse doctrines that are far from Orthodox Islam. For example, they classify all White people as "devils."

• *Ideologies of Empowerment*

Around 1900, W. E. B. DuBois proposed Black solidarity through education. He saw the need for African Americans to pull together as a cultural nation, demand their rights, and deal with their situation from a position of militant education and strength.

The next great movement in this area was the New Negro Movement, also known as the Harlem Renaissance, which lasted from about 1910 to 1940. It consisted of expressions against racism and social injustice through the creative arts.

In 1965, Black Nationalism was espoused by Malcolm X. At the time Malcolm proposed this, it did not catch on that widely. However, in 1967, two years after the death of Malcolm, the Black Consciousness Movement hit the scene and was quite influential. This movement was, in essence, the popularization of Black Nationalism. The Black Consciousness Movement had several sub-phases to it, including Black Awareness, Black Power, Black Revolution, and neo-Pan-Africanism.

A DIMINISHED ROLE

The Black militants denounced the theology of suffering. For most of the twentieth century, it had been applied to coping with racism rather than resisting it. Thus, they viewed the African American church as an instrument of Black pacification.

This all changed when Rev. Martin Luther King Jr. transformed the theology of suffering into a powerful spiritual weapon to overcome injustice and segregation. Under his leadership, the theology of suffering empowered the Civil Rights Movement from 1955 to 1968.

However, by 1967 the call for Black Consciousness arose and the Civil Rights Movement was seen as irrelevant. The Black militants wrongly confused desegregation with assimilation into the dominant White culture. For them, assimilation nullified the African American core cultural values, namely, human dignity, African identity, and the significance of the Black experience. Of course, these militants never recognized the core cultural values they cherished were themselves the products of Christian theology (the theology of empowerment).

When the Black militants turned away from the Word of God, they turned away from the only valid basis for the Black ethnicity they were trying to develop. For them, the only strategies Christianity had to offer were coping and assimilation. These strategies were seen as part of the White agenda to keep Black people "in their place." Christianity was therefore dubbed "the White man's religion" and incompatible with Black Consciousness.

This is why these militant thinkers excluded Christian values from the matrix of Black thought. Although incorrectly identified as Christianity, it was White "Christianity-ism" that was bitterly denounced by the militants, and is still denounced today. As the Black Consciousness Movement gained influence, the traditional African American church suffered a diminished role in twentieth century society.

Chapter 9

New Models of African American Churches

"Therefore, my dear brothers, stand firm. Let nothing move you. Always give yourselves fully to the work of the Lord, because you know that your labor in the Lord is not in vain" (1 Corinthians 15:58, NIV).

CHANGING WITH THE TIMES

When W. E. B. Dubois called for Black solidarity through education, he was too far ahead of his time. In 1900 formal education was beyond the reach of most African Americans. However, as the twentieth century progressed, academics became an increasing fixture in our culture. This meant that more of us began to develop the cognitive side of our intelligence. Unfortunately, African American theology remained oriented to the intuitive side. Thus, as the influence of academic institutions increased, theological influence of the church tended to decrease. To reverse this trend, a cognitive theology was needed.

In response to these changing times, new models of African American churches emerged. Three of these models were the evangelical, the charismatic, and the prosperity. Like the traditional models, these three were also culturally non-transformative. A fourth model thus far seems to be developing a more transformative outlook—the dominion model.

• *The Evangelical Model*

The evangelical model emerged in the mid-1930s. Up to this time, there was a significant evangelical presence among immigrants from the Caribbean. Because they tended to stay to themselves, evangelicalism had a marginal influence among African Americans at best. Things began to change with the ministry of three immigrant brothers from the Bahamas: Whitfield Nottage, T. B. Nottage, and B. M. Nottage. They intentionally reached beyond the boundaries of the Afro-Caribbean community to minister to African Americans. Their ministry was a major factor in the emergence of African American evangelicals.

Churches in this movement were based on cognitive theology and emphasized analytical knowledge. Because this theology developed in a White context, it tends to be limited to the scope of dominant cultural concerns. Thus, these churches generally followed the characteristics of their White counter parts. This movement was associated with what they called the "fundamentals of the faith," including the inspiration and inerrancy of the Scriptures, the virgin birth of Christ, the deity of Christ, and so on.

Preoccupied with private salvation, the evangelical model often opposed any social involvement in the community. The thought was, "Why bother to polish the brass or rearrange the furniture on the Titanic?" They thought their job was solely to get people onto the lifeboat of salvation and depend upon God to take care of everything in the millennial kingdom. Because of the White cultural influence, the evangelical church model tended to be indifferent to African American core cultural concerns.

However, these churches shared a keen interest in foreign missions. But this interest was not inspired by the great African American missions movement prior to the twentieth century. After all, they had no knowledge of it. By the mid-1930s, the traditional church had totally forgotten its missions history. Since these evangelicals had no appreciation for intuitive theology, they viewed the traditional church as "apostate" and "not missions-minded."

African American evangelicals who sensed a "call" to foreign missions faced a major roadblock. Almost all White missions agencies refused to consider their applications. In response to this, several interdenominational missions agencies were set up. Some of these included:

1. The Afro-American Missionary Crusade, founded in Philadelphia, Pennsylvania, in 1949
2. Carver Foreign Missions, founded in Atlanta, Georgia, in 1955
3. Have Christ Will Travel, founded in Philadelphia, Pennsylvania, in 1965

Thus, missions involvement in the African American church began to flicker again.

• *The Charismatic Model*
The charismatic model emerged in the late 1960s. It was also based on cognitive theology and shared most of the cultural limitations of the evangelical movement.

The early history of the charismatic movement helped to set its cultural agenda. It began with the 1906–1909 Azusa Street Revival in Los Angeles, California. The movement that emerged from this Pentecostal outbreak was racially integrated but under Black leadership. Within a few years, Whites withdrew from this movement. The charismatic movement developed from this schism. Eventually, these White Charismatics began to reach African Americans. This was the birth of the Black Charismatic movement. Its theological outlook was a preoccupation not only with private salvation, but also with personal spiritual experiences. Because of the cultural limitations it inherited, this model tended to be indifferent to African American core cultural concerns.

Partially inspired by their evangelical counterparts, Black charismatic churches began to show an interest in missions. Part of this interest can also be explained by their view that the "baptism in the Holy Spirit" was a new move of God to bring a great revival to the church in these "last days."

• *The Prosperity Model*

The prosperity model emerged in the mid-1970s. Based on cognitive theology, it also followed the cultural characteristics of its White counterpart. Those who initially formulated this theology did so from a White dominant cultural perspective. Its theological outlook was a preoccupation with private salvation and personal well-being. Because prosperity theology shared the same cultural limitations as the previous nontraditional models, it also tended to be indifferent to African American cultural core concerns.

By the late 1990s, these churches began to develop a missions consciousness. Their reasoning was as follows:

1. God wants us to prosper.
2. However, our prosperity should not be only for prosperity sake.
3. We must use our prosperity to be a blessing to others in the world, namely, missions involvement.

• *The Dominion Model*

The dominion model emerged as a glimmer of hope in the late 1980s. Though it is based on cognitive theology, it does not follow a White agenda. Neither does it follow the agenda set forth by the Black Consciousness Movement. Its theological outlook focuses on personal salvation, casting a vision of *Kingdom empowerment* and missions. In fact, dominion churches have combined the best characteristics of the traditional and nontraditional African American church models. While the nontraditional churches kept the idea of global missions alive, the dominion churches have been on the vanguard of the general reawakening to African American participation in The Great Commission of Jesus Christ.

These churches also address many contemporary African American core cultural concerns. However, they have yet to develop a theology of *Kingdom transformation* or a fully functioning biblical world and life view that would make this transformation possible.

This model has given us further glimpses into where the African American church needs to be, but like all the church models, it still has a long way to go.

LONGING TO HEAR THE GOSPEL

Traditionally, African American theology had been more concerned with issues related to how we should obey God (ethics) than with issues related to what we should know about God (epistemology). These new models focused primarily on what we should know about God. The evangelical, charismatic, and prosperity models were oriented to the dominant White culture. Therefore, they proved to be incapable of addressing our core cultural concerns. Many times they even served to anesthetize us to these concerns.

While the importance of personal salvation should never be diminished, salvation must extend beyond the private realm. The Bible never sets up a dichotomy between personal salvation and social action. The call of the church is to make disciples of every nation to the glory of God (Matthew 28:18–20).

If we're going to see the church coming to its own in the twenty-first century, we need an authentic African American cognitive theology that focuses on what we should know about God *and* how we should obey God—a theology that extensively addresses our core cultural concerns today. In addition, this theology must interface with our historic intuitive theology, and it must contribute to the global church.

There are an amazing number of people in the world who are longing to hear the Gospel from African Americans, given what we've been through. I believe that God has called us to be a people who would carry the Gospel to the ends of the earth in these last days. We must move beyond ourselves, open our eyes, and look at the "fields," for they are ripe for harvest (John 4:35).

Chapter 10

Let's Get Busy

"'Do not think that because you are in the king's house you alone . . . will escape. For if you remain silent at this time, relief and deliverance...will arise from another place.... And who knows but that you have come to royal position for such a time as this?'"
(Esther 4:13–14, NIV).

As we celebrated the arrival of the twenty-first century, many of us looked back on how things had changed over the previous 100 years. While it is obvious that African Americans have made great strides, it is evident that not all the changes we have witnessed were positive. Today, the church seems to retain a considerable influence. For example, regular church attendance for African Americans is significantly higher than for Whites. The popularity of gospel music is growing more rapidly than for most other musical genre. Encouraging as this may be, it cannot hide the fact that we are in the midst of a great cultural crisis—a crisis that has taken our eyes off the divine significance of the African American experience.

COLD WAR

At the turn of the twentieth century, most African Americans were poor sharecroppers in the rural South. Soon after World War I, another great Black migration began; it continued into the early 1970s. Like the migration in the late 1800s, this one brought African Americans to the urban North in search of a better way of life. Because of housing segregation, almost all Black people in the North were confined to overcrowded ghettos. Some in the ghetto ("the hood") lived by values that generally led to success in life in spite of the obstacles of institutional racism. They became the "haves." Most others who did not live by these values generally ended up in poverty and depravation. They became the "have-nots."

Conditions in the hood at that time may not have been ideal, but there was a sense of community. The "haves" felt an obligation to help the "have-nots" by instilling in them values to help them prosper. This all began to change in the mid-1960s with three significant developments: (1) the end of housing discrimination—a result of the Civil Rights Movement; (2) the dramatic rise of gang violence in the ghetto; and (3) the widening of the lifestyle gap, which led to an increase in resentment of the "have-nots" toward the "haves." (The "have-nots" never saw any real benefit from the Civil Rights or Black Consciousness Movements while the "haves" did.)

The result of these developments was a migration of the "haves" from the ghetto, leaving the "have-nots" behind to cope with the deteriorating conditions in the hood. This migration was complete by the mid-1980s. Not only did it diminish the African American sense of community, it led to a complete separation between those who were prosperous and those who were poor. Without the influence of those who were successful, the culture of the hood degenerated into one of chaos, dysfunctional behavior, and death. "Gangsta" rap became the voice of this ghetto culture. Today the "haves" and "have-nots" virtually have nothing in common. In fact, there is a cold war between these two.

Both groups have lost sight of the divine significance of the African American experience—the "haves" because of the lure of materialism ("bling bling") and the "have-nots" because of the impact of the thug mentality. Although the culture of the "haves" may be the *majority* African American subculture, the culture of the "have-nots" has become the *dominant* subculture. Thus, the thug mentality exerts the greatest influence on the emerging generations of both groups. This is a manifestation of the cultural crisis we face today.

INTERFACE

The African American church was unable to adequately address these and other issues because it operated on theology that was culturally non-transformative. One hundred years ago, the church's influence in our culture was theological. Today our influence is primarily stylistic. The historic empowerment concerns of dignity, identity, and significance are still with us. However, the emergence of the ghetto subculture has given us additional core cultural concerns related to dysfunction. These issues include pain, rage, and a quest for true manhood.

After the mid-1960s, Christian input was largely absent from the developing Black Consciousness Movement. Because of this, non-Christians are best known for having articulated the core concerns related to empowerment and dysfunction. Malcolm X is revered as the spokesman for the empowerment concerns, and Tupac Shakur voiced the dysfunction concerns.

Malcolm X burst upon the popular scene at the height of the Civil Rights Movement in the early 1960s. He challenged the prevailing assumptions that the racial divide would soon be bridged through desegregation. For Malcolm, moral persuasion through non-violent demonstrations would not end the institutional racism he faced. For 12 years, he was a dedicated leader in the Nation of Islam and a devoted disciple of Elijah Muhammad. He gained his greatest popularity after his break with the Nation. As a self-styled "Black Nationalist," he championed the empowerment values of dignity, identity, and significance. Toward the end of his life, Malcolm became more conciliatory toward those with whom he disagreed. However, he was not able to complete his spiritual journey. He was assassinated in Harlem, New York, in 1965 at the age of 39.

In the early 1990s, Tupac Shakur began to emerge onto the "hip-hop" scene as a member of the group Digital Underground. His solo CD, *2Pacalypse Now*, catapulted him to prominence as a "gangsta" rapper in a genre of music known for its frequent references to cop killing and sexual violence. His haunting lyrics were fraught with themes of dysfunction. The depth of Tupac's rap made him stand out from his peers. In 1998, at the age of 25, Tupac's life was cut short when he was shot to death in Las Vegas, Nevada. He became an even bigger star after his death with the release of several more of his CDs. In fact, in the eyes of many, he has become the ideal thug and the embodiment of the thug mentality.

By the late 1960s, Black and liberation theologians attempted to address the cultural concerns Malcolm X identified. These theologians were trying to show how Black ideology could be expressed in theological language. In the 1990s, others tried to address the issues articulated by

Tupac Shakur. While these theologies provided some valuable insights, they were not widely embraced by the African American church. The new theologies did not interface very well with the intuitive theology of the traditional church, nor did they interface with the cognitive theology of the non-traditional church. Thus, the church tended to view these theologies with suspicion.

I believe we can do better in this century with the theological approach discussed in chapter 6. Now is the time for a fresh theology that is biblically sound and culturally transformative—a theology that addresses our cultural core concerns. Now is the time for the church to reestablish its theological influence. By a faithful application of God's Word to our core concerns, we will get the attention of our emerging generations. Their ability to see the kingdom of God will dramatically improve. A generation transformed by the holistic Gospel of Jesus Christ will make a huge difference in the African American community and beyond. Therefore, we will begin to rediscover the significance of our presence in this country.

A NEHEMIAH VISION

The global church is anxious to hear from African American Christians. They want to know how the Gospel was able to speak to us and sustain us through our experience of oppression. They are longing to know the story behind how "God has made a way out of no way." Truly, we have a great story to tell, but too many of us have forgotten how God has worked through our history. This has hindered our ability to meet today's challenges. The cold war (between the prosperous and poor) and the thug mentality have crippled our capacity to participate in the global cause of God's kingdom. We must begin to correct this situation by restoring our sense of community—not only for our sakes, but also for the sake of The Great Commission.

If we follow Christ, we must not become apathetic about today's cultural crisis. We must counter the thug mentality with a Nehemiah vision. Nehemiah was a gifted young man described in the Bible as the "wine taster" for King Artaxerxes I of Persia. Nehemiah did far more than taste wines for poison; he held a powerful position in the palace as the king's close companion and advisor. He also determined who would have access to the king. He was like the "chief of staff" for the White House. Nehemiah's career success did not lead to spiritual failure, nor did it cause him to forget the oppression of his people (the "have-nots") back in Jerusalem ("the hood"). The Bible tells us that he used the resources at his disposal to liberate and empower his people.

Like Nehemiah and like the founders of the Free African Society, we need to develop ways to do practical theology that both brings people to Christ and moves us to improve the quality of life through community development. We must rediscover and update the theology of empowerment.

GOING GLOBAL

Three weeks after my first book was published in 1983, I received an enthusiastic letter from a minister in New Zealand. He expressed how insights he gained from the book revolutionized his ministry. I was delighted to receive his letter but was a bit confused by his response. I had no idea that a book about the Black American experience had anything to say in New Zealand. When we met the following year, I asked him how a book about Black folks could have helped him so much. His response was, "I am a Maori." The puzzled look on my face prompted him to explain, "We are the native people of New Zealand. The dynamics between us and the English settlers is the same as between Black Americans and Whites."

One week later, another letter arrived from a prominent leader in South Africa who would play a pivotal role in that country's transition from apartheid to freedom. He enclosed the transcript of his keynote speech to a national racial reconciliation conference. About eight of the twelve pages of the manuscript were quotations from my book.

It was then that I realized I was going global without even trying. From that time, I have been on an amazing journey of discovery as my awareness of the global body of Christ has grown. In my international travels, I have been struck by the tremendous cultural influence African Americans have had through music (R & B, jazz, blues, gospel, and so on). It is astonishing to see how people throughout the world seem to have positive feelings toward African Americans. Could this influence and favor be God-given?

BE READY

This postmodern era has ushered in a host of new megatrends. For example, the center of gravity in the body of Christ is shifting away from America and the West. This has ground-shaking implications. The church in the West is declining, while the church in Africa, Asia, and South America is emerging. The African American church today faces a great choice that will influence its direction for the rest of this century. With whom will we identify, the declining church or the emerging church?

Today the trend is away from national structures (e.g., denominations, missions agencies) to local/global partnerships. As I pointed out in chapter 3, many African American churches have begun to develop these relationships. We cannot afford to continue to let this happen haphazardly. We must intentionally raise the consciousness of our fellow African American Christians to the enormous missions opportunities God has laid before us.

The global favor we have is no accident. It is time to show our gratitude to God for His saving grace by seeking to glorify Him through global outreach. But where do we begin? Here are some suggestions:

1. We should pray for God to give us a vision for the nations.

2. We should learn as much as we can about the nations God lays on our hearts. A good resource is *Operation World: 21st Century Edition,* by Patrick Johnstone and Jason Mandryk.

3. We should seek short-term missions opportunities, whether here or abroad, or help others to do so.

4. We should be open to God's leading on how we can be a part of the emerging African American missions movement.

You also must be ready, because the Son of man will come at an hour when you do not expect Him (Matthew 24:44).

So let's get busy!

Selected Bibliography

Berry, L. L. *A Century of Missions of the African Methodist Episcopal Church.* New York, N.Y.: Gutenberg Printing Company, 1942.

Crummell, Alexander. *The Future of Africa.* New York, N.Y.: Negro Universities Press, 1969.

Ellis, Carl F. *Free At Last?: The Gospel in the African-American Experience.* Downers Grove, Ill.: InterVarsity Press, 1996.

Frame, John M. *The Doctrine of God.* Phillipsburg, N.J.: P & R Publishing Company, 2002.

Frame, John M. *The Doctrine of the Knowledge of God.* Phillipsburg, N.J.: P & R Publishing Company, 1989.

Johnstone, Patrick, and Jason Mandryk. *Operation World: 21st Century Edition.* Carlisle, Cumbria, United Kingdom: Paternoster Publishing, 2001.

Keener, Craig S., and Glenn Usry. *Defending Black Faith.* Downers Grove, Ill.: InterVarsity Press, 1997.

Knowles, Louis L., and Kenneth Prewitt, eds. *Institutional Racism in America.* Englewood Cliffs, N.J.: Prentice Hall, 1969.

Mitchell, Henry. *Black Preaching: The Recovery of a Powerful Art.* New York, N.Y.: HarperSanFrancisco, 1979.

Selected Bibliography

Payne, Daniel A. *A History of the African Methodist Episcopal Church*. New York, N.Y.: Johnson Reprint Corp., 1968.

Salley, Columbus. *The Black 100: A Ranking of the Most Influential African-Americans, Past and Present* (Revised and Updated). New York, N.Y.: Kensington Publishing Corporation, 2001.

Salley, Columbus, and Ronald Behm. *What Color is Your God?* Downers Grove, Ill.: InterVarsity Press, 1981.

Sernett, Milton C., ed. *African American Religious History: A Documentary Witness*. Durham, N.C.: Duke University Press, 2000.

Usry, Glenn, and Craig S. Keener. *Black Man's Religion*. Downers Grove, Ill.: InterVarsity Press, 1996.

Williams, Walter L. *Black Americans and the Evangelization of Africa: 1877–1900*. Madison, Wis.: University of Wisconsin Press, 1982.

Woodson, Carter G., ed. *Negro Orators and Their Orations*. New York, N.Y.: Russell & Russell Publishing Company, 1969.